Easy Air Fryer Recipes

Have Fun in the Kitchen and Learn to Fry, Bake, Grill and Roast with Your Air Fryer

Linda Wang

© **Copyright 2021 by Linda Wang - All rights reserved.**

The content contained within this book may not be reproduced, duplicated or transmitted without direct written permission from the author or the publisher.
Under no circumstances will any blame or legal responsibility be held against the publisher, or author, for any damages, reparation, or monetary loss due to the information contained within this book. Either directly or indirectly.

Legal Notice:
This book is copyright protected. This book is only for personal use. You cannot amend, distribute, sell, use, quote or paraphrase any part, or the content within this book, without the consent of the author or publisher.

Disclaimer Notice:
Please note the information contained within this document is for educational and entertainment purposes only. All effort has been executed to present accurate, up to date, and reliable, complete information. No warranties of any kind are declared or implied. Readers acknowledge that the author is not engaging in the rendering of legal, financial, medical or professional advice. The content within this book has been derived from various sources. Please consult a licensed professional before attempting any techniques outlined in this book.
By reading this document, the reader agrees that under no circumstances is the author responsible for any losses, direct or indirect, which are incurred as a result of the use of information contained within this document, including, but not limited to, — errors, omissions, or inaccuracies.

TABLE OF CONTENTS

INTRODUCTION 1

Cinnamon Pudding 5

Raspberries Oatmeal 7

Green Beans Sauté 9

Creamy Green Beans and Tomatoes 10

Roasted Potatoes with Garlic and Bacon 12

Easy Pesto Gnocchi 13

Homemade Falafel Burger 15

Kale Chips 17

Herbed Radish Sauté 18

Roasted Potatoes & Yogurt 19

Delicious French Fries 21

Roasted Brussels Sprouts 23

Prawn Burgers 25

Crispy Scallops 27

Honey & Sriracha Tossed Calamari 29

Teriyaki Glazed Halibut Steak 31

Awesome Shrimp Mix 33

Spicy Cod 34

Simple Turkey Breast 35

Creamy Chicken Tenders 37

- Mushroom Chicken 39
- Pepper Chicken 41
- Lemongrass Chicken 43
- Chicken Burger Patties 45
- Simple Beef Burgers 46
- Oregano Pork Chops 48
- Lamb Chops and Dill 50
- Pork Chops and Spinach 52
- Cinnamon Beef 54
- Pork Neck Salad 56
- Glazed Ham 59
- Herbed Leg of Lamb 61
- Broccoli and Tomatoes Air Fried Stew 63
- Kale and Brussels Sprouts 65
- Zucchini and Olives 67
- Creamy Kale 68
- Air fryer Angel Hair Soup 70
- Green Chicken Chili 72
- Carrot Soup with Fowl 75
- Manchow Soup 77
- Teriyaki Grilled Chicken 79
- Grilled Turmeric and Lemongrass Chicken .. 81
- Peruvian Grilled Chicken 83

Almond Cupcakes 85

Plum Cake 87

Fruity Oreo Muffins 89

Apple Bread Pudding 91

Coffee Flavored Doughnuts 93

Vanilla Soufflé 95

Lemon Chocolate Cookies 98

NOTES 100

INTRODUCTION

An Air Fryer is a magic revolutionized kitchen appliance that helps you fry with less or even no oil at all. This kind of product applies Rapid Air technology, which offers a new way to fry with less oil. This new invention cooks food through the circulation of superheated air and generates 80% low-fat food. Although the food is fried with less oil, you don't need to worry as the food processed by the Air Fryer still has the same taste like the food fried using the deep-frying method.

This technology uses a superheated element, which radiates heat close to the food and an exhaust fan in its lid to circulate airflow. An Air Fryer ensures that the food processed is cooked completely. The exhaust fan located at the top of the cooking chamber helps the food get the same heating temperature in every part quickly, resulting in a cooked food of better and healthier quality. Besides, cooking with an Air Fryer is also suitable for those individuals which are too busy or do not have enough time. For example, an Air Fryer only needs half a spoonful of oil and takes 10 minutes to serve a medium bowl of crispy French fries.

In addition to serving healthier food, an Air Fryer also provides some other benefits to you. Since an Air Fryer helps you fry using less oil or without oil for some kind of food, it automatically reduces the fat and cholesterol content in food. Indeed, no one will refuse to enjoy fried food without worrying about the greasy and fat content. Having fried food with no guilt is one of the pleasures of life. Besides having low fat and cholesterol, you save some amount of money by consuming oil sparingly, which can be used for other needs. An Air Fryer also can reheat your food. Sometimes, when you have fried leftover and you reheat it, it will usually serve reheated greasy food with some addition of unhealthy reuse oil. Undoubtedly, the saturated fat in the fried food gets worse because of this process. An Air Fryer helps you reheat your food without being afraid of extra oils that the food may absorb. Fried bananas, fish and chips, nuggets, or even fried chicken can be reheated to become as warm and crispy as they were before by using an Air Fryer.

Some people may think that spending some amount of money to buy a fryer is wasteful. I dare to say that they are wrong because an Air Fryer is not only used to fry. It is a sophisticated multi-function appliance since it also helps you to roast chicken, make steak, grill fish, and even bake a cake. With a built-in air filter, an Air Fryer filters the air and saves your kitchen from smoke and grease.

An air Fryer is really a new innovative method of cooking. Grab it fast and welcome to a clean and healthy kitchen.

Cinnamon Pudding

Preparation Time: 16 minutes

Servings: 2

Ingredients:

- 4 eggs; whisked
- 2 tbsp. heavy cream
- 4 tbsp. erythritol
- ½ tsp. cinnamon powder

- ¼ tsp. allspice, ground
- Cooking spray

Directions:

1. Take a bowl and mix all the ingredients except the cooking spray, whisk well and pour into a ramekin greased with cooking spray
2. Add the basket to your Air Fryer, put the ramekin inside and cook at 400 °F for 12 minutes. Divide into bowls and serve for breakfast.

Nutrition:

Calories: 201; Fat: 11g; Fiber: 2g; Carbs: 4g; Protein: 6g

Raspberries Oatmeal

Preparation Time: 20 minutes

Servings: 4

Ingredients:

- ½ cups raspberries
- 1 ½ cups coconut; shredded
- 2 cups almond milk
- ¼ tsp. nutmeg, ground
- 2 tsp. stevia
- ½ tsp. cinnamon powder
- Cooking spray

Directions:

1. Grease the air fryer's pan with cooking spray, mix all the ingredients inside, cover and cook at 360 °F for 15 minutes. Divide into bowls and serve

Nutrition:

Calories: 172; Fat: 5g; Fiber: 2g; Carbs: 4g; Protein: 6g

Green Beans Sauté

Preparation Time: 10 minutes

Cooking time: 20 minutes

Servings: 4

Ingredients:

- 2 pounds green beans, trimmed and halved
- 1 tablespoon balsamic vinegar
- 1 tablespoon dill, chopped
- 2 tablespoons olive oil
- Salt and black pepper to the taste

Directions:

1. In your air fryer's basket, combine the green beans with the vinegar and the other Ingredients, toss and cook at 350 degrees F for 20 minutes.
2. Divide between plates and serve as a side dish.

Nutrition:

Calories 133, fat 3, fiber 8, carbs 16, protein 3

Creamy Green Beans and Tomatoes

Preparation Time: 10 minutes

Cooking time: 20 minutes

Servings: 4

Ingredients:

- 1 pound green beans, trimmed and halved
- ½ pound cherry tomatoes, halved
- 2 tablespoons olive oil

- 1 teaspoon basil, dried
- 1 teaspoon oregano, dried
- 1 cup heavy cream
- Salt and black pepper to the taste
- ½ tablespoon cilantro, chopped

Directions:

1. In your air fryer's pan, combine the green beans with the tomatoes and the other Ingredients, toss and cook at 360 degrees F for 20 minutes.
2. Divide the mix between plates and serve.

Nutrition:

Calories 174, fat 5, fiber 7, carbs 11, protein 4

Roasted Potatoes with Garlic and Bacon

Preparation Time: 40 minutes

Servings: 2

Ingredients:

- 4 strips bacon; chopped
- 4 potatoes; peeled and cut into bite-size chunks
- 6 cloves garlic; unpeeled
- 1 tablespoon fresh rosemary; finely chopped

Directions:

1. In a large bowl; combine the potatoes, garlic, bacon, and rosemary and mix thoroughly. Transfer to a baking dish.
2. Briefly preheat your Air Fryer to 350 - degrees Fahrenheit. Cook the potatoes in the Fryer until golden brown; 25 – 30 minutes.

Easy Pesto Gnocchi

Preparation Time: 30 minutes

Servings: 3

Ingredients:

- 1 package [16-ounce] shelf-stable gnocchi
- 1 medium-sized onion; chopped
- 3 garlic cloves; minced

- 1/3 cup Parmesan cheese; grated
- 1 jar [8 ounce] pesto
- 1 tablespoon extra-virgin olive oil
- salt and black pepper; to taste

Directions:

1. In the large mixing bowl combine onion, garlic, and gnocchi and sprinkle with the olive oil. Stir to combine.
2. Preheat the Air Fryer to 340 - degrees Fahrenheit. Cook for 15 – 20 minutes; stirring couple time while cooking, until gnocchi are lightly browned and crisp.
3. Stir in the pesto and Parmesan cheese.
4. Serve immediately.

Homemade Falafel Burger

Preparation Time: 35 minutes

Servings: 5

Ingredients:

- 14 ounces. can chickpeas
- 1 small lemon
- 1 small red onion
- 5 ounces. gluten free oats
- 2 tablespoon cheese
- 2 tablespoon feta cheese
- 4 tablespoon soft cheese
- 3 tablespoon greek yoghurt
- 1 tablespoon garlic puree
- 1 tablespoon coriander
- 1 tablespoon oregano
- 1 tablespoon parsley
- salt & pepper to taste

Directions:

1. Place in a food processor or blender all the seasonings, the garlic, the lemon rind, red onion and the drained chickpeas. Whiz until they are coarse but not smooth.
2. Mix them in bowl with 1/2 the soft cheese, the hard cheese and the feta.
3. Combine them into burger shapes.
4. Roll them in gluten free oats until you cannot see any of the chickpea mixture. Place them in the Air Fryer inside the Air Fryer baking pan and cook for 8 minutes at 360 - degrees Fahrenheit.
5. Make the burger sauce. In a mixing bowl add the rest of the soft cheese, the Greek Yoghurt and some extra salt and pepper.
6. Mix well until it is nice and fluffy. Add the juice of the lemon and mix one last time.
7. Place the falafel burger inside your homemade buns with garnish.
8. Load up with your burger sauce.

Kale Chips

Preparation Time: 10 minutes

Servings: 4

Ingredients:

- 4 cups stemmed kale
- 2 tsp. avocado oil
- ½ tsp. salt

Directions:

1. Take a large bowl, toss kale in avocado oil and sprinkle with salt. Place into the air fryer basket.
2. Adjust the temperature to 400 Degrees F and set the timer for 5 minutes. Kale will be crispy when done. Serve immediately.

Nutrition:

Calories: 25; Protein: 0.5g; Fiber: 0.4g; Fat: 2.2g; Carbs: 1.1g

Herbed Radish Sauté

Preparation Time: 20 minutes

Servings: 4

Ingredients:

- 2 bunches red radishes; halved
- 2 tbsp. parsley; chopped.
- 1 tbsp. olive oil
- 2 tbsp. balsamic vinegar
- Salt and black pepper to taste.

Directions:

1. Take a bowl and mix the radishes with the remaining ingredients except the parsley, toss and put them in your air fryer's basket.
2. Cook at 400 °F for 15 minutes, divide between plates, sprinkle the parsley on top and serve as a side dish

Nutrition:

Calories: 180; Fat: 4g; Fiber: 2g; Carbs: 3g; Protein: 5g

Roasted Potatoes & Yogurt

Preparation Time: 55 minutes

Servings: 3

Ingredients:

- Pounds potatoes [waxy]
- 1 tablespoon paprika [spicy]
- black pepper [freshly ground] to taste
- 1 tablespoon olive oil
- salt to taste
- ounces. yoghurt [Greek]

Directions:

1. Preheat Air Fryer at 350 – degrees Fahrenheit.
2. Peel and cut potatoes in small pieces of about 3 cm cubes, soak the pieces in cold water for 30 minutes.
3. After 30 minutes' drain and pat dry the potato pieces.

4. In a medium size bowl add 1 tablespoon. of oil, paprika and sprinkle pepper and stir well. Coat the cubes with the mixture.
5. Put in fryer and air fry for about 20 minutes. Serve them with dip or pari-pari sauce. Enjoy the delicious combination.

Delicious French Fries

Preparation Time: 25 minutes

Servings: 3

Ingredients:

- 6 medium russet potatoes; peeled
- 2 tablespoon olive oil

Directions:

1. Peel the potatoes and cut them into 1/4 inch by 3-inch strips.
2. Soak the potatoes in water for at least 30 minutes; then drain thoroughly and pat dry with a paper towel.
3. Preheat the Air Fryer to 360 - degrees Fahrenheit.
4. Place the potatoes in a large bowl and mix in oil, coating the potatoes lightly. Add the potatoes to the cooking basket and cook for 30 minutes or until golden brown and crisp. Shake 2 – 3 times during cooking.
5. Tip: Thicker cut potatoes will take longer to cook; while thinner cut potatoes will cook faster.

Roasted Brussels Sprouts

Preparation Time: 30 minutes

Servings: 3

Ingredients:

- 2 cups Brussels sprouts
- 1 orange [juice and zest]
- 1/4 cup pine nuts [toasted]
- 1/4 raisins [drained]

- 1 tablespoon oil [olive]

Directions:

1. Preheat Air Fryer to 390 – degrees Fahrenheit.
2. Boil sprouts for about 4 minutes and then put them in cold water and drain the sprouts properly.
3. Meanwhile; soak raisins in orange juice for 15 minutes. Now roast the cooled sprouts with oil for 15 minutes. Serve with nuts, raisins and zest.

Prawn Burgers

Preparation Time: 20 minutes

Cooking Time: 6 minutes

Servings: 2

Ingredients:

- ½ cup prawns, peeled, deveined and finely chopped
- 2-3 tablespoons onion, finely chopped
- ½ cup breadcrumbs
- 3 cups fresh baby greens
- ½ teaspoon garlic, minced
- ½ teaspoon ginger, minced
- ½ teaspoon red chili powder
- ½ teaspoon ground cumin
- ¼ teaspoon ground turmeric
- Salt and ground black pepper, as required

Directions:

1. Preheat the Air fryer to 390 degrees F and grease an Air fryer basket.
2. Mix the prawns, breadcrumbs, onion, ginger, garlic, and spices in a bowl.
3. Make small-sized patties from the mixture and transfer to the Air fryer basket.
4. Cook for about 6 minutes and dish out in a platter.
5. Serve immediately warm alongside the baby greens.

Nutrition:

Calories: 240, Fat: 2.7g, Carbohydrates: 37.4g, Sugar: 4g, Protein: 18g, Sodium: 371mg

Crispy Scallops

Preparation Time: 15 minutes

Cooking Time: 6 minutes

Servings: 4

Ingredients:

- 18 sea scallops, cleaned and patted very dry
- ½ egg
- 1/8 cup all-purpose flour
- 1 tablespoon 2% milk
- ¼ cup cornflakes, crushed
- ½ teaspoon paprika
- Salt and black pepper, as required

Directions:

1. Preheat the Air fryer to 400 degrees F and grease an Air fryer basket.
2. Mix flour, paprika, salt, and black pepper in a bowl.

3. Whisk egg with milk in another bowl and place the cornflakes in a third bowl.
4. Coat each scallop with the flour mixture, dip into the egg mixture and finally, dredge in the cornflakes.
5. Arrange scallops in the Air fryer basket and cook for about 6 minutes.
6. Dish out the scallops in a platter and serve hot.

Nutrition:

Calories: 150, Fat: 1.7g, Carbohydrates: 8g, Sugar: 0.4g, Protein: 24g, Sodium: 278mg

Honey & Sriracha Tossed Calamari

Preparation time: 25 minutes

Servings: 1-2

Ingredients:

- Calamari tubes - tentacles if you prefer: .5 lb.
- Club soda: 1 cup
- Flour: 1 cup
- Salt - red pepper & black pepper: 2 dashes each
- Honey: .5 cup+ 1-2 tbsp. Sriracha
- Red pepper flakes: 2 shakes

Directions:

1. Fully rinse the calamari and blot it dry using a bunch of paper towels. Slice into rings: .25-inch wide). Toss the rings into a bowl. Pour in the club soda and stir until all are submerged. Wait for about 10 minutes.
2. Sift the salt, flour, red & black pepper. Set aside for now.

3. Dredge the calamari into the flour mixture and set on a platter until ready to fry.
4. Spritz the basket of the Air Fryer with a small amount of cooking oil spray. Arrange the calamari in the basket, careful not to crowd it too much.
5. Set the temperature at 375º Fahrenheit and the timer for 11 minutes.
6. Shake the basket twice during the cooking process, loosening any rings that may stick.
7. Remove from the basket, toss with the sauce, and return to the fryer for two more minutes.
8. Serve with additional sauce as desired.
9. Make the sauce by combining honey, sriracha, and red pepper flakes in a small bowl, mix until fully combined.

Teriyaki Glazed Halibut Steak

Preparation time: 20 minutes

Servings: 3

Ingredients:

- Halibut steak: 1 lb.

Ingredients - The Marinade:

- Low-sodium soy sauce: .66 cup
- Mirin Japanese cooking wine: .5 cup

- Orange juice: .25 cup
- Sugar: .25 cup
- Lime juice: 2 tbsp.
- Ground ginger: .25 tsp.
- Crushed red pepper flakes: .25 tsp.
- Smashed garlic: 1 clove

Directions:

1. Warm the Air Fryer at 390º Fahrenheit.
2. Mix all of the marinade fixings in a saucepan, bringing it to a boil. Lower the heat setting to medium and cool.
3. Pour half of the marinade in a plastic bag with the halibut and zip it closed. Marinate in the refrigerator for about 30 minutes.
4. Air fry the halibut for 10-12 minutes. Brush using the remaining glaze over the steak.
5. Serve with a bed of rice. Add a little basil or mint or basil for extra flavoring.

Awesome Shrimp Mix

Preparation Time: 20 minutes

Servings: 4

Ingredients:

- 18 oz. shrimp; peeled and deveined
- 2 green chilies; minced
- 1 tsp. turmeric powder
- 1 tbsp. olive oil
- 2 onions; chopped.
- 4 oz. curd; beaten
- 1-inch ginger; chopped.
- 1/2 tbsp. mustard seeds
- Salt and black pepper to taste

Directions:

1. In a pan that fits your air fryer, place and mix all the ingredients.
2. Place the pan in the fryer and cook at 380 °F for 10 minutes. Divide into bowls and serve

Spicy Cod

Preparation Time: 15 minutes

Servings: 4

Ingredients:

- 4 cod fillets; boneless
- 1 lemon; sliced
- 2 tbsp. assorted chili peppers
- Juice of 1 lemon
- Salt and black pepper to taste

Directions:

1. In your air fryer, mix the cod with the chili pepper, lemon juice, salt and pepper
2. Arrange the lemon slices on top and cook at 360°F for 10 minutes. Divide the fillets between plates and serve.

Simple Turkey Breast

Preparation Time: 20 minutes

Cooking Time: 40 minutes

Servings: 10

Ingredients:

- 1: 8-poundsbone-in turkey breast
- 2 tablespoons olive oil
- Salt and black pepper, as required

Directions:

1. Preheat the Air fryer to 360 degrees F and grease an Air fryer basket.
2. Season the turkey breast with salt and black pepper and drizzle with oil.
3. Arrange the turkey breast into the Air Fryer basket, skin side down and cook for about 20 minutes.
4. Flip the side and cook for another 20 minutes.
5. Dish out in a platter and cut into desired size slices to serve.

Nutrition:

Calories: 719, Fat: 35.9g, Carbohydrates: 0g, Sugar: 0g, Protein: 97.2g, Sodium: 386mg

Creamy Chicken Tenders

Preparation Time: 15 minutes

Cooking Time: 20 minutes

Servings: 8

Ingredients:

- 2 pounds chicken tenders
- 1 cup feta cheese
- 1 cup cream
- 4 tablespoons olive oil
- Salt and black pepper, to taste

Directions:

1. Preheat the Air fryer to 340 degrees F and grease an Air fryer basket.
2. Season the chicken tenders with salt and black pepper.
3. Arrange the chicken tenderloins in the Air fryer basket and drizzle with olive oil.\

4. Cook for about 15 minutes and set the Air fryer to 390 degrees F.
5. Cook for about 5 more minutes and dish out to serve warm.
6. Repeat with the remaining mixture and dish out to serve hot.

Nutrition:

Calories: 344, Fat: 21.1g, Carbohydrates: 1.7g, Sugar: 1.4g, Protein: 35.7g, Sodium: 317mg

Mushroom Chicken

Preparation time: 10-20,

Cooking time: 15-30;

Serve: 6

Ingredients:

- 500 g chicken breast
- Mushroom 300g
- 100 g of fresh cream

- 1 shallot

Direction:

1. Cut the chicken into pieces and sliced mushrooms. Spray the basket and chopped shallot into the basket. Set the temperature to 150 °C and lightly brown for 5 minutes.
2. Add the mushrooms and cook for additional 6 minutes.
3. Finally, pour the chicken, salt, pepper, and simmer for another 10 minutes.
4. Then add the fresh cream and cook for 5 min. until the sauce has thickened.

Nutrition:

Calories 220, Fat 14g, Carbohydrates 11g, Sugar 4g, Protein 12g, Cholesterol 50mg

Pepper Chicken

Preparation time: 10-20;

Cooking time: 45-60;

Serve: 6

Ingredients:

- 1 kg of chicken pieces
- 500 g of red and yellow peppers
- 50g onion

- Salt to taste

Direction:

1. Pour the chopped onion into the bowl with the chopped peppers and chicken. Add salt and pepper.
2. Set the temperature to 150 ^{0}C.
3. Cook everything for about 50 minutes, mixing 3 to 4 times during cooking, both meat and peppers.

Nutrition:

Calories 281, Fat 12g, Carbohydrates 21g, Sugars 3.4g, Protein 23g, Cholesterol 102mg

Lemongrass Chicken

Preparation Time: 40 minutes

Servings: 4

Ingredients:

- 10 chicken drumsticks
- 1 bunch lemongrass; trimmed
- 1 cup coconut milk
- 1/4 cup parsley; chopped.
- 1 yellow onion; chopped.
- 3 tbsp. soy sauce
- 2 tbsp. fish sauce
- 1 tsp. butter; melted
- 1 tbsp. ginger; chopped.
- 4 garlic cloves; minced
- 1 tbsp. lemon juice
- Salt and black pepper to taste

Directions:

1. In a blender, combine the lemongrass, ginger, garlic, soy sauce, fish sauce and coconut milk; pulse well.
2. Put the butter in a pan that fits your air fryer and heat it up over medium heat; add the onions, stir and cook for 2-3 minutes
3. Add the chicken, salt, pepper and the lemongrass mix; toss well
4. Place the pan in the fryer and cook at 380°F for 25 minutes
5. Add the lemon juice and the parsley and toss. Divide everything between plates and serve.

Chicken Burger Patties

Cooking Time: 11 minutes

Servings: 1

Ingredients:

- 1-2 chicken patties.

Directions:

1. Preheat air fryer at 360 °F for 3 minutes. Place the frozen chicken patties into the basket and cook for 11 minutes. Serve as desired

Simple Beef Burgers

Preparation Time: 20 minutes

Cooking Time: 12 minutes

Servings: 6

Ingredients:

- 2 pounds ground beef
- 12 dinner rolls
- 12 cheddar cheese slices
- 6 tablespoons tomato ketchup
- Salt and black pepper, to taste

Directions:

1. Preheat the Air fryer to 390 degrees F and grease an Air fryer basket.
2. Mix the beef, salt and black pepper in a bowl.
3. Make small equal-sized patties from the beef mixture and arrange half of the patties in the Air fryer basket.

4. Cook for about 12 minutes and top each patty with 1 cheese slice.
5. Arrange the patties between rolls and drizzle with ketchup.
6. Repeat with the remaining batch and dish out to serve hot.

Nutrition:

Calories: 537, Fat: 28.3g, Carbohydrates: 7.6g, Sugar: 4.2g, Protein: 60.6g, Sodium: 636mg

Oregano Pork Chops

Preparation Time: 20 minutes

Servings: 4

Ingredients:

- 4 pork chops
- 2 tbsp. oregano; chopped.
- 4 garlic cloves; minced
- 2 tbsp. olive oil
- Salt and black pepper to taste

Directions:

1. Place all of the ingredients in a bowl and toss / mix well
2. Transfer the chops to your air fryer's basket and cook at 400 °F for 15 minutes. Serve with a side salad and enjoy!

Lamb Chops and Dill

Preparation Time: 30 minutes

Servings: 6

Ingredients:

- 1 lb. lamb chops
- 2 yellow onions; chopped.
- 2 tbsp. sweet paprika
- 1 tbsp. olive oil

- 2 tbsp. dill; chopped.
- 3 cups chicken stock
- 1½ cups heavy cream
- 1 garlic clove; minced
- Salt and black pepper to taste

Directions:

1. Put the lamb chops in your air fryer and season with the salt, pepper, garlic and paprika; rub the chops thoroughly
2. Cook at 380 °F for 10 minutes
3. Transfer the lamb to a baking dish that fits your air fryer. Then add the onions, stock, cream and dill and toss.
4. Place the pan in the fryer and cook everything for 7-8 minutes more. Divide everything between plates and serve hot

Pork Chops and Spinach

Preparation Time: 20 minutes

Servings: 4

Ingredients:

- 2 pork chops
- 3 tbsp. spinach pesto
- 1/4 cup beef stock
- 2 cups baby spinach
- Salt and black pepper to taste

Directions:

1. Place the pork chops, salt, pepper and spinach pesto in a bowl; toss well
2. Place the pork chops in the air fryer and cook at 400 °F for 4 minutes on each side.
3. Transfer the chops to a pan that fits your air fryer and add the stock and the baby spinach
4. Put the pan in the fryer and cook at 400 °F for 7 minutes more. Divide everything between plates and serve.

Cinnamon Beef

Preparation Time: 60 minutes

Servings: 6

Ingredients:

- 2 lbs. beef roast
- 2 garlic cloves; minced
- 2 yellow onions; thinly sliced

- 1 cup beef stock
- Juice of 1 lemon
- 1 tbsp. cilantro; chopped.
- 1½ tbsp. cinnamon powder
- Salt and black pepper to taste

Directions:

1. In a baking dish that fits your air fryer, mix the roast with all other ingredients and toss well.
2. Place the dish in your fryer and cook at 390 °F for 55 minutes, flipping the roast halfway
3. Carve the roast, divide between plates and serve with the cooking juices drizzled on top; enjoy!

Pork Neck Salad

Servings: 2

Preparation Time: 20 minutes

Cooking Time: 12 minutes

Ingredients

For Pork:

- ½ pound pork neck
- 1 tablespoon soy sauce
- 1 tablespoon fish sauce
- ½ tablespoon oyster sauce

For Salad:

- 1 ripe tomato, thickly sliced
- 1 scallion, chopped
- 1 red onion, sliced
- 1 bunch fresh basil leaves
- 1 bunch fresh cilantro leaves

For Dressing:

- 3 tablespoons fish sauce

- 2 tablespoons olive oil
- 1 teaspoon apple cider vinegar
- 1 tablespoon palm sugar
- 1 bird eye chili
- 1 tablespoon garlic, minced

Directions:

1. For pork: in a bowl, mix together all the sauces.
2. Add the pork neck and generously coat with marinade.
3. Refrigerate for about 2-3 hours.
4. Set the temperature of air fryer to 340 degrees F. Grease an air fryer basket.
5. Place pork neck into the prepared basket.
6. Air fry for about 12 minutes.
7. Meanwhile, for the salad: in a serving bowl, mix together all the ingredients.
8. For dressing: in another bowl, add all the ingredients and beat until well combined.

9. Remove pork neck from air fryer and cut into desired size slices.
10. Place the pork slices over salad.
11. Add the dressing and toss to coat well.
12. Serve.

Nutrition:

Calories: 448, Carbohydrate: 15.2g, Protein: 20.5g, Fat: 39.7g, Sugar: 8.5g, Sodium: 2000mg

Glazed Ham

Servings: 4

Preparation Time: 15 minutes

Cooking Time: 40 minutes

Ingredients

- 1 pound 10½ ounces ham
- 2 tablespoons French mustard
- 1 cup whiskey
- 2 tablespoons honey

Directions:

1. Place the ham at room temperature for about 30 minutes before cooking.
2. In a bowl, mix together the whiskey, mustard, and honey.
3. Place the ham in a baking dish that fits in the air fryer.
4. Top with half of the honey mixture and coat well.

5. Set the temperature of air fryer to 320 degrees F. Place the baking dish into the air fryer.
6. Air fry for about 15 minutes.
7. Flip the side of ham and top with the remaining honey mixture.
8. Air fry for about 25 more minutes.
9. Remove from air fryer and place the ham onto a platter for about 10 minutes before slicing.
10. Cut the ham into desired size slices and serve.

Nutrition:

Calories: 558, Carbohydrate: 18.6g, Protein: 43g, Fat: 22.2g, Sugar: 8.7g, Sodium: 3000mg

Herbed Leg of Lamb

Servings: 5

Preparation Time: 10 minutes

Cooking Time: 75 minutes

Ingredients

- 2 pounds bone-in leg of lamb
- 2 tablespoons olive oil
- 2 fresh rosemary sprigs
- 2 fresh thyme sprigs
- Salt and ground black pepper, as required

Directions:

1. Coat the leg of lamb with oil and sprinkle with salt and black pepper.
2. Wrap the leg of lamb with herb sprigs.
3. Set the temperature of air fryer to 300 degrees F. Grease an air fryer basket.
4. Place leg of lamb into the prepared air fryer basket.

5. Air fry for about 75 minutes.
6. Remove from air fryer and transfer the leg of lamb onto a platter.
7. With a piece of foil, cover the leg of lamb for about 10 minutes before slicing.
8. Cut the leg of lamb into desired size pieces and serve.

Nutrition:

Calories: 534, Carbohydrate: 2.4g, Protein: 69.8g, Fat: 25.8g, Sugar: 0g, Sodium: 190mg

Broccoli and Tomatoes Air Fried Stew

Preparation Time: 10 minutes

Cooking duration: 20 minutes

Servings: 4

Ingredients:

- 1 broccoli head, florets separated
- 2 teaspoons coriander seeds
- 1 yellow onion, chopped
- 1 tablespoon olive oil
- 1 small ginger piece, chopped
- 1 garlic clove, minced
- 28 ounces canned tomatoes, pureed
- Salt and black pepper to the taste
- A pinch of red pepper, crushed

Directions:

1. Heat up a pan that fits your air fryer with the oil over medium heat, add onions, salt, pepper and red pepper, stir and cook for 7 minutes.

2. Add ginger, garlic, coriander seeds, tomatoes and broccoli, stir, introduce in your air fryer and cook at 360 °F for 12 minutes.
3. Divide into bowls and serve.

Nutrition:

Calories: 150; Fat: 4g; Fiber: 2g; Carbs: 4g; Protein: 5g

Kale and Brussels Sprouts

Preparation Time: 20 minutes

Servings: 8

Ingredients:

- 1 lb. Brussels sprouts, trimmed
- 3 oz. mozzarella, shredded
- 2 cups kale, torn
- 1 tbsp. olive oil

- Salt and black pepper to taste.

Directions:

1. In a pan that fits the air fryer, combine all the Ingredients: except the mozzarella and toss.
2. Put the pan in the air fryer and cook at 380 °F for 15 minutes
3. Divide between plates, sprinkle the cheese on top and serve.

Nutrition:

Calories: 170; Fat: 5g; Fiber: 3g; Carbs: 4g; Protein: 7g

Zucchini and Olives

Preparation Time: 17 minutes

Servings: 4

Ingredients

- 4 zucchinis; sliced
- 2 tbsp. olive oil
- 2 tsp. balsamic vinegar
- 1 cup kalamata olives, pitted
- 2 tbsp. lime juice
- Salt and black pepper to taste.

Directions:

1. In a pan that fits your air fryer, mix the olives with all the other ingredients, toss, introduce in the fryer and cook at 390 °F for 12 minutes
2. Divide the mix between plates and serve.

Nutrition:

Calories: 150; Fat: 4g; Fiber: 2g; Carbs: 4g; Protein: 5g

Creamy Kale

Preparation Time: 20 minutes

Servings: 4

Ingredients

- 2 lb. kale, torn
- 2 garlic cloves; minced
- ½ cup parmesan, grated
- ½ tsp. nutmeg, ground
- 1 ½ cups coconut cream
- 2 tbsp. olive oil
- A pinch of salt and black pepper

Directions:

1. In a pan that fits your air fryer, mix the kale with the rest of the ingredients, toss, introduce the pan in the fryer and cook at 400 °F for 15 minutes.
2. Divide between plates and serve

Nutrition:

Calories: 135; Fat: 3g; Fiber: 2g; Carbs: 4g; Protein: 6g

Air fryer Angel Hair Soup

Preparation Time: 5 minutes

Cooking Time: 15 minutes

Servings: 4

Ingredients:

- 4 Cups of low sodium chicken broth
- 3 Tbsp of tomato sauce
- ½ lb of angel hair pasta
- 7 leaves of fresh basil
- ¼ Cup of parmesan cheese to serve
- 2 tbsp of olive oil
- 2 Peeled and diced carrots
- 1 Peeled and cubed potato
- ¼ Cup of chickpeas

Directions:

1. Pour the oil, and add the broth, the chickpeas, the carrots, the tomato sauce and the basil in your Air fryer

2. Press sauté and let the ingredients simmer for around 5 minutcs.
3. Add 1 and ½ cup of chicken broth or and close the lid of the Air fryer.
4. Set at high pressure for around 10 minutes.
5. Once the timer beeps, quick release the pressure and stir in the angel's hair pasta.
6. Boil the ingredients for 5 minutes
7. Add the basil and let cook for another minute.
8. Serve in bowl with a sprinkle of Parmesan cheese and tortilla strips.
9. Serve and enjoy!

Nutrition:

Calories – 216 Protein – 12.4 g. Fat – 3.8 g. Carbs – 35.1 g.

Green Chicken Chili

Preparation Time: 10 minutes

Cooking Time: 35 minutes

Servings: 8

Ingredients:

- 2 tbsp. unsalted butter
- 1 medium yellow onion (to be peeled and chopped)
- ½ lb. poblano peppers (to be seeded and roughly chopped)
- ½ lb. Anaheim peppers (to be seeded and roughly chopped)
- ½ lb. tomatillos (to be husked and quartered)
- 2 small jalapeño peppers (to be seeded and roughly chopped)
- 2 garlic cloves (to be peeled and minced)
- 1 tsp. ground cumin
- 6 bone-in, skin-on chicken thighs (2 ½ lbs. in total)
- 2 cups chicken stock

- 2 cups water
- 1/3 cup roughly chopped fresh cilantro
- 3 cans Great Northern beans (to be drained and rinsed, 15 oz. cans)

Directions:

1. Choose the "Sauté" button on the Air fryer and when hot, add butter to melt. Once the butter melts, add onion and cook for about 3 minutes until softened. Add poblano and Anaheim peppers, then tomatillos, and jalapeños. Cook 3 minutes add garlic and cumin. Cook about 30 seconds or until fragrant. Then cancel sautéing.

2. Add the thighs, stock, and water to pot and stir. Tightly close lid and have the steam release set to the "Sealing" position. Select the "Rice/Grain" option and set the timer for 30 minutes. At the end of the cook time, do a quick release of pressure and open lid to stir well. Press the "Cancel" button and transfer the chicken to a cutting board. After carefully removing the skin, shred the meat with two forks.

3. Using an immersion blender, purée the sauce until smooth. Stir in the meat, cilantro, and beans and serve warm.

Nutrition:

Calories – 304 Protein – 33 g. Fat – 10 g. Carbs – 19 g.

Carrot Soup with Fowl

Preparation Time: 8 minutes

Cooking Time: 20 minutes

Servings: 4

Ingredients:

- ½ fowl or chicken
- 2 quarts of chicken broth
- ¼ Cup of coarsely chopped onion
- 1 Teaspoon of saffron threads
- ½ Cup of coarsely chopped carrots
- ½ Cup of coarsely chopped celery
- ¾ Cup of corn kernels
- ½ Cup of finely chopped celery
- 1 tablespoon of fresh chopped parsley
- 1 Cup of cooked egg noodles

Directions:

1. Start by combining all together the stewing chicken or fowl with the chicken broth in your Air fryer

2. Press sauté and add the onions, the carrots, the celery and the saffron
3. Now, close the lid and set at high pressure for around 20 minutes
4. Once the timer beeps, remove the chicken and shred it from the bone and cut it into small pieces
5. Strain your saffron broth with a fine sieve and then add the celery, the corn, the parsley, and the cooked noodles to your broth.
6. Return your soup to simmer for a few minutes
7. Serve and enjoy a delicious and nutritious soup

Nutrition:

Calories – 154.4 Protein – 10.9 g. Fat – 0.8 g. Carbs – 27.2 g.

Manchow Soup

Preparation Time: 10 minutes

Cooking Time: 25 minutes

Servings: 4

Ingredients:

- ½ cup green bell peppers
- 3 oz. fried noodles, for garnish
- ½ cup bean sprouts
- ½ cup mushrooms
- ½ cup broccoli
- ½ cup baby carrots
- 2 green onions, chopped
- 4 garlic cloves, minced
- ½ inch ginger, minced
- 1 teaspoon soy sauce
- 2 teaspoons chilli sauce
- 1 teaspoon vinegar
- 3 cups vegetable stock
- 1 tablespoon oil
- Salt and pepper, to taste

- Roasted crushed peanuts, for garnish

Directions:

1. Put the oil, ginger, garlic, carrots, onions and carrots in the Air fryer and select "Sauté".
2. Sauté for 4 minutes and add soy sauce, chilli sauce, vinegar and vegetable stock.
3. Set the Air fryer to "Soup" and cook for 10 minutes at high pressure.
4. Release the pressure naturally and add cooked noodles.
5. Season with salt and black pepper and garnish with fried noodles and crushed roasted peanuts.

Nutrition:

Calories: 379; Total Fat: 20.8g; Carbs: 43.6g; Sugars: 2.4g; Protein: 8.7g

Teriyaki Grilled Chicken

Servings: 3

Cooking Time: 40 minutes

Ingredients:

- ½ cup soy sauce
- ½ cup water
- 3 tablespoons brown sugar
- 3 cloves of garlic, minced
- 1 tablespoon minced ginger
- 3 tablespoon honey
- 1 tablespoons rice vinegar
- 3 tablespoons olive oil
- 1 ½ pounds boneless skinless chicken breasts

Directions

1. Place all ingredients in a Ziploc bag and give a good shake. Allow marinating in the fridge for at least 2 hours.
2. Preheat the air fryer at 375 degrees F.
3. Place the grill pan accessory in the air fryer.

4. Grill the chicken for 40 minutes making sure to flip the chicken every 10 minutes.
5. Meanwhile, prepare the teriyaki glaze by pouring the marinade on a saucepan and allow to simmer over medium flame until the sauce thickens.
6. Before serving, brush the chicken with the teriyaki glaze.

Nutrition

Calories: 603; Carbs: 33.7g; Protein: 54.4g; Fat: 27.3g

Grilled Turmeric and Lemongrass Chicken

Servings: 6

Cooking Time: 40 minutes

Ingredients:

- 3 shallots, chopped
- 3 cloves of garlic, minced
- 2 lemongrass stalks
- 1 teaspoon turmeric
- 2 tablespoons fish sauce
- 3 pounds whole chicken
- Salt and pepper to taste

Directions

1. Place all ingredients in a Ziploc bag and allow to marinate for at least 2 hours in the fridge.
2. Preheat the air fryer at 375 degrees F.
3. Place the grill pan accessory in the air fryer.
4. Grill the chicken for 40 minutes making sure to flip every 10 minutes for even grilling.

Nutrition

Calories: 486; Carbs: 49.1g; Protein: 38.5g; Fat: 16.1g

Peruvian Grilled Chicken

Servings: 4

Cooking Time: 40 minutes

Ingredients:

- 1/3 cup soy sauce
- 2 tablespoons fresh lime juice
- 2 teaspoons ground cumin
- 5 cloves of garlic, minced
- 1 teaspoon paprika
- ½ teaspoon dried oregano
- 2 ½ pounds chicken, quartered

Directions

1. Place all ingredients in a Ziploc bag and shake to mix everything.
2. Allow marinating for at least 2 hours in the fridge.
3. Preheat the air fryer at 375 degrees F.

4. Place the grill pan accessory in the air fryer.
5. Grill the chicken for 40 minutes making sure to flip the chicken every 10 minutes for even grilling.

Nutrition

Calories:389; Carbs: 7.9g; Protein: 59.7g; Fat: 11.8g

Almond Cupcakes

Preparation Time: 5 minutes

Cooking time: 25 minutes

Servings: 4

Ingredients:

- 1/3 cup coconut flour
- 4 eggs, whisked
- ½ cup cocoa powder

- 3 tablespoons stevia
- ½ teaspoon baking soda
- 1 teaspoon baking powder
- 1 teaspoon vanilla extract
- 4 tablespoons coconut oil, melted
- ¼ cup almond milk
- Cooking spray

Directions:

1. In a bowl, mix all the Ingredients: except the cooking spray and whisk well.
2. Grease a cupcake tin that fits the air fryer with the cooking spray, pour the cupcake mix, put the pan in your air fryer, cook at 350 degrees F for 25 minutes, cool down and serve.

Nutrition:

Calories 103, fat 4, fiber 2, carbs 6, protein 3

Plum Cake

Preparation Time: 40 minutes

Servings: 8

Ingredients:
- 4 plums, pitted and chopped.
- 3 eggs
- ½ cup coconut flour
- 1 ½ cups almond flour
- ¾ cup almond milk

- ½ cup butter, soft
- ½ cup swerve
- 1 tbsp. vanilla extract
- 2 tsp. baking powder
- ¼ tsp. almond extract

Directions:

1. Take a bowl and mix all the ingredients and whisk well.
2. Pour this into a cake pan that fits the air fryer after you've lined it with parchment paper, put the pan in the machine and cook at 370 °F for 30 minutes.
3. Cool the cake down, slice and serve

Nutrition:

Calories: 183; Fat: 4g; Fiber: 3g; Carbs: 4g; Protein: 7g

Fruity Oreo Muffins

Preparation Time: 15 minutes

Cooking Time: 10 minutes

Servings: 6

Ingredients:

- 1 cup milk
- 1 pack Oreo biscuits, crushed
- ¾ teaspoon baking powder
- 1 banana, peeled and chopped
- 1 apple, peeled, cored and chopped
- 1 teaspoon honey
- 1 teaspoon cocoa powder
- 1 teaspoon fresh lemon juice
- A pinch of ground cinnamon

Directions:

1. Preheat the Air fryer to 320 degrees F and grease 6 muffin cups lightly.
2. Mix milk, biscuits, cocoa powder, baking soda, and baking powder in a bowl until well

combined.
3. Transfer the mixture into the muffin cups and cook for about 10 minutes.
4. Remove from the Air fryer and invert the muffin cups onto a wire rack to cool.
5. Meanwhile, mix the banana, apple, honey, lemon juice, and cinnamon in another bowl.
6. Scoop some portion of muffins from the center and fill with fruit mixture to serve.

Nutrition:

Calories: 182, Fat: 3.1g, Carbohydrates: 31.4g, Sugar: 19.5g, Protein: 3.1g, Sodium: 196mg

Apple Bread Pudding

Preparation Time: 59 minutes

Servings: 8

Ingredients:

For Bread Pudding:

- 10½-oz bread, cubed
- 1/4 cup walnuts; chopped
- 1 ½ cups milk
- 1/2 cup raisins
- 3/4 cup water
- 1/2 cup apple, peeled, cored and chopped
- 5 tbsp. honey
- 2 tsp. ground cinnamon
- 2 tsp. cornstarch
- 1 tsp. vanilla extract

For Topping:

- 3/5 cup brown sugar
- 1 ⅓ cups plain flour
- 7 tbsp. butter

Directions:

1. In a large bowl; mix well bread, apple, raisins and walnuts. In another bowl, add the remaining pudding ingredients and mix until well combined. Add the milk mixture into bread mixture and mix until well combined. Refrigerate for about 15 minutes, tossing occasionally
2. For topping: in a bowl; mix together the flour and sugar. With a pastry cutter, cut in the butter until a crumbly mixture forms. Set the temperature of air fryer to 355 °F
3. Place the mixture evenly into 2 baking pans and spread the topping mixture on top of each. Place 1 pan into an air fryer basket. Air fry for about 22 minutes. Repeat with the remaining pan. Remove from the air fryer and serve warm.

Coffee Flavored Doughnuts

Servings: 6

Cooking Time: 6 minutes

Ingredients

- ¼ cup coconut sugar
- ¼ cup coffee
- ½ teaspoon salt
- 1 tablespoon sunflower oil
- 1 cup white all-purpose flour
- 1 teaspoon baking powder
- 2 tablespoon aquafaba

Directions:

1. In a mixing bowl mix together the dry Ingredients flour, sugar, salt, and baking powder.
2. In another bowl, combine the aquafaba, sunflower oil, and coffee.
3. Mix to form a dough.

4. Let the dough rest inside the fridge.
5. Preheat the air fryer to 400 degrees F.
6. Knead the dough and create doughnuts.
7. Arrange inside the air fryer in a single layer and cook for 6 minutes.
8. Do not shake so that the donut maintains its shape.

Nutrition:

Calories: 113; Carbohydrates: 20.45g; Protein: 2.16g; Fat:2.54g

Vanilla Soufflé

Servings: 6

Preparation Time: 15 minutes

Cooking Time: 39 minutes

Ingredients

- ¼ cup butter, softened
- ¼ cup all-purpose flour
- 1 cup milk
- 4 egg yolks
- 5 egg whites
- ½ cup plus 2 tablespoons sugar, divided
- 3 teaspoons vanilla extract, divided
- 1 teaspoon cream of tartar
- 2 tablespoons powdered sugar plus extra for dusting

Directions:

1. In a bowl, add the butter, and flour and mix until a smooth paste forms.
2. In a medium pan, mix together ½ cup of sugar and milk over medium-low heat and cook for

about 3 minutes or until the sugar is dissolved, stirring continuously.
3. Add the flour mixture, whisking continuously and simmer for about 3-4 minutes or until mixture becomes thick.
4. Remove from the heat and stir in 1 teaspoon of vanilla extract.
5. Set aside for about 10 minutes to cool.
6. In a bowl, mix together the egg yolks and 1 teaspoon of vanilla extract.
7. Add the egg yolk mixture into milk mixture and mix until well combined.
8. In another bowl, add the egg whites, cream of tartar, remaining sugar, and vanilla extract and whisk until stiff peaks form.
9. Fold the egg whites mixture into milk mixture.
10. Set the temperature of air fryer to 330 degrees F. Grease 6 ramekins and sprinkle each with a pinch of sugar.
11. Place mixture evenly into the prepared ramekins and with the back of a spoon, smooth the top surface.

12. Arrange the ramekins into an air fryer basket in 2 batches.
13. Air fry for about 14-16 minutes.
14. Remove from air fryer and set aside to cool slightly.
15. Sprinkle with the powdered sugar and serve warm.

Nutrition:

Calories: 250, Carbohydrate: 29.8g, Protein: 6.8g, Fat: 11.6g, Sugar: 25g, Sodium: 107mg

Lemon Chocolate Cookies

Servings: 4

Preparation Time: 15 minutes

Cooking Time: 5 minutes

Ingredients:

- 1 cup almond flour
- 1 egg yolk
- 6 tablespoons butter
- 4 tablespoons Stevia
- ½ cup semi-sweet chocolate chips

Directions

1. Place butter and stevia in a mixing bowl then using an electric mixer beat until fluffy.
2. Add egg yolk to the bowl then continue beating until incorporated.
3. Stir almond flour into the mixture then using a wooden spatula mix until becoming dough.
4. Add chocolate chips to the dough then mix until just combined.

5. Preheat an Air Fryer to 180 °F (82°C).
6. Shape the dough into small ball forms, then arrange in the Air Fryer.
7. Press the cookie balls until becoming coin forms then cook in the Air Fryer for 5 minutes.
8. Once it is done, remove from the Air Fryer then place on a cooling rack. Let them cool.
9. Serve and enjoy.

Nutrition Values:

Net Carbs: 5.4g; Calories: 246; Total Fat: 23.9g; Saturated Fat: 12.6g

Protein: 2.9g; Carbs: 6.7g

Notes

www.ingramcontent.com/pod-product-compliance
Lightning Source LLC
Chambersburg PA
CBHW070935080526
44589CB00013B/1524